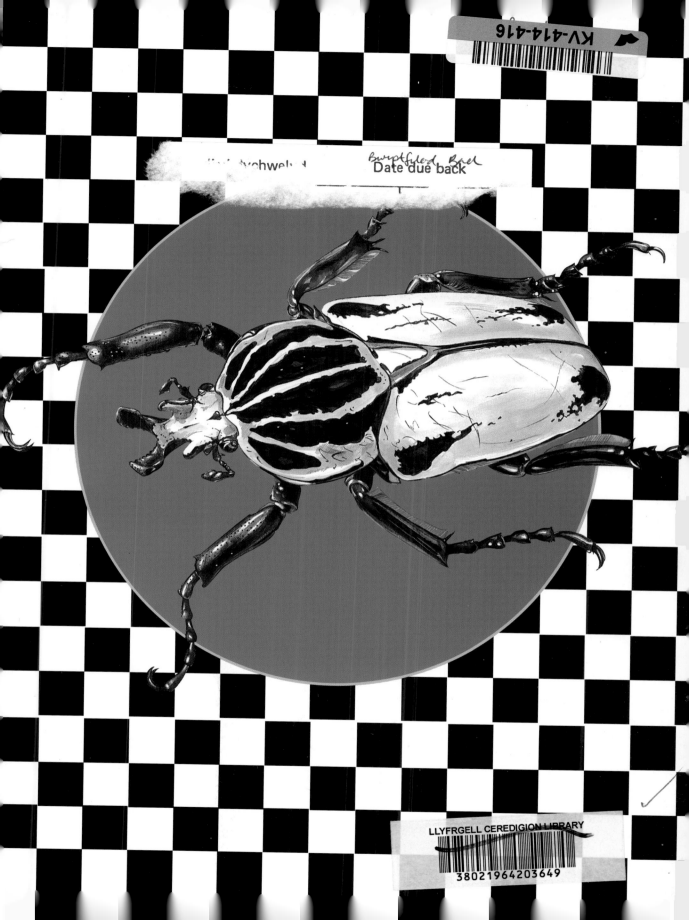

Kathryn Senior is a former biomedical research scientist who studied at Cambridge University, England for a degree in pathology and a doctorate in microbiology. After four years in research she joined the world of publishing as an editor of children's science books. She is the author of several books, including **Medicine** in the *Timelines* series and **Rainforest** in the *Fast Forward* series. Dr Senior is now a freelance writer and editor.

Illustrators: Carolyn Scrace
Nick Hewetson
Pam Hewetson
Dave Antram

David Salariya was born in Dundee, Scotland. He has designed and created the award-winning *Timelines*, *New View*, *X-Ray Picture Book* and *Inside Story* series and many other books for publishers in the UK and abroad. He lives in Brighton with his wife, the illustrator Shirley Willis, and their son Jonathan.

Editor: Karen Barker Smith

© The Salariya Book Company Ltd
MCMXCIX

Created, designed and produced by

THE SALARIYA BOOK COMPANY LTD
25 Marlborough Place,
Brighton BN1 1UB

ISBN 0 7500 2726 6

Published in 1999 by
MACDONALD YOUNG BOOKS
an imprint of Wayland Publishers Ltd
61 Western Road
Hove BN3 1JD

You can find Macdonald Young Books on the internet at http://www.myb.co.uk

A CIP catalogue record for this book is available from the British Library.

Printed in Hong Kong.

CHECKERS
SUPERBUGS
& MINIBEASTS

Written by Kathryn Senior

Created & Designed by David Salariya

MACDONALD YOUNG BOOKS

$\mathcal{C}$ontents

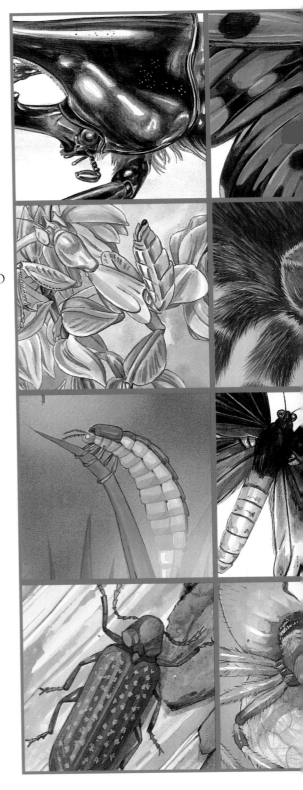

Arthropods are a group of animals whose bodies are divided into segments. They all have tough outer skeletons. They are sub-divided according to their features (see below).

What are bugs?

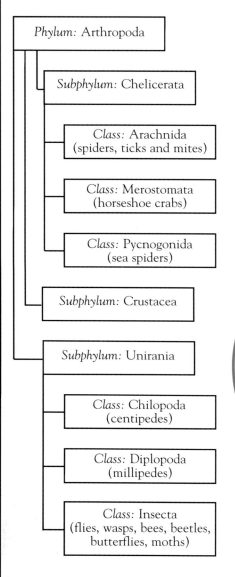

Phylum: Arthropoda

Subphylum: Chelicerata

Class: Arachnida
(spiders, ticks and mites)

Class: Merostomata
(horseshoe crabs)

Class: Pycnogonida
(sea spiders)

Subphylum: Crustacea

Subphylum: Unirania

Class: Chilopoda
(centipedes)

Class: Diplopoda
(millipedes)

Class: Insecta
(flies, wasps, bees, beetles, butterflies, moths)

Which are the biggest, the fastest, the longest, the smallest, the noisiest, the most dangerous and the most revolting super-bugs and minibeasts? The bugs in this book are not all insects but they are all arthropods. It's a good idea to know what the difference is. The diagram on the left shows how the group of animals called arthropods is divided up. There are several sub-groups. This book concentrates on Arachnida (spiders, ticks and mites), Chilopoda (centipedes), Diplopoda (millipedes) and Insecta (insects). Insects include flies, wasps, bees, beetles, dragonflies, butterflies and moths. Let's start by having a closer look at the main characteristics of arachnids and insects.

larva

pupa

Ladybird
life cycle

adult

Some insects, ladybirds, for example, look different at different stages of their life cycle. They experience what is called complete metamorphosis. They start life as an egg, which hatches into a larva. The larva then grows, shedding its skin several times as it gets bigger. Then, at the crucial moment, the larva changes into a pupa. A few days later an adult ladybird emerges.

Other insects, such as this flower bug (right), just get bigger at each stage of life, shedding their skin each time. This type of life cycle is called incomplete metamorphosis, because the change is gradual, rather than sudden. The egg develops into a larva, called a nymph. The nymph sheds its skin as it gets bigger. Finally, it becomes an adult.

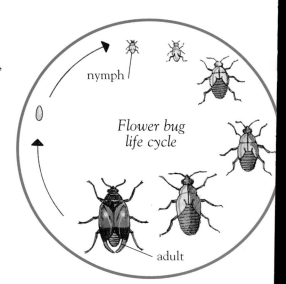

nymph

Flower bug
life cycle

adult

Factfile: Thousands of species
• The phylum Arthropoda (arthro = joint, poda = foot) is the largest phylum in the animal kingdom. It includes about 75% of all species.
• 900,000 species of arthropods have been identified. Many more have yet to be studied.
• The oldest fossil insect is a 390-million year old bristletail found in Quebec, Canada.

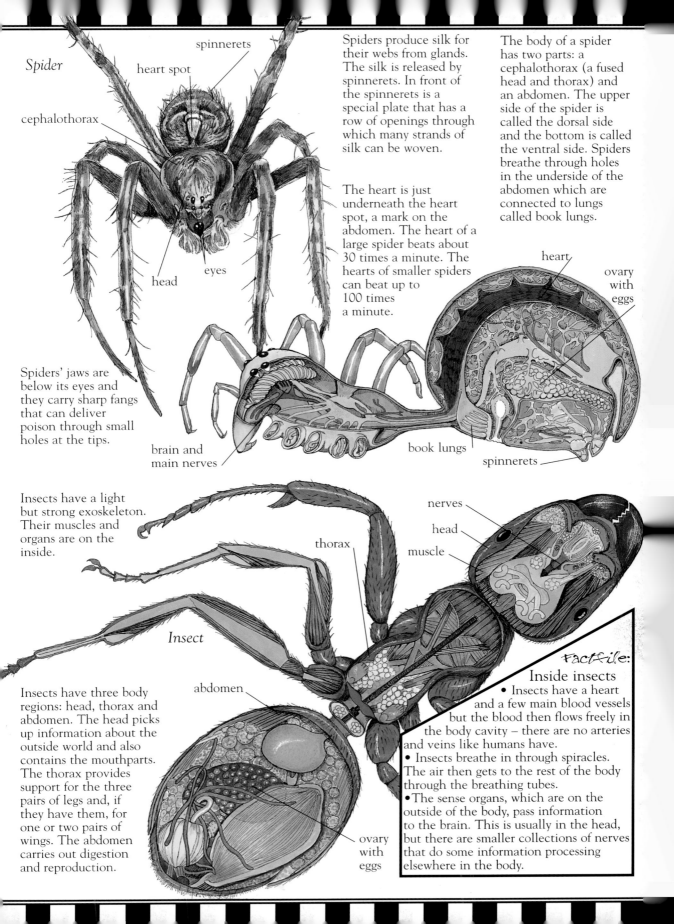

Spider

spinnerets

heart spot

cephalothorax

head

eyes

Spiders produce silk for their webs from glands. The silk is released by spinnerets. In front of the spinnerets is a special plate that has a row of openings through which many strands of silk can be woven.

The heart is just underneath the heart spot, a mark on the abdomen. The heart of a large spider beats about 30 times a minute. The hearts of smaller spiders can beat up to 100 times a minute.

The body of a spider has two parts: a cephalothorax (a fused head and thorax) and an abdomen. The upper side of the spider is called the dorsal side and the bottom is called the ventral side. Spiders breathe through holes in the underside of the abdomen which are connected to lungs called book lungs.

Spiders' jaws are below its eyes and they carry sharp fangs that can deliver poison through small holes at the tips.

brain and main nerves

book lungs

heart

ovary with eggs

spinnerets

Insects have a light but strong exoskeleton. Their muscles and organs are on the inside.

Insect

thorax

nerves

head

muscle

abdomen

Insects have three body regions: head, thorax and abdomen. The head picks up information about the outside world and also contains the mouthparts. The thorax provides support for the three pairs of legs and, if they have them, for one or two pairs of wings. The abdomen carries out digestion and reproduction.

ovary with eggs

Factfile:
Inside insects
• Insects have a heart and a few main blood vessels but the blood then flows freely in the body cavity – there are no arteries and veins like humans have.
• Insects breathe in through spiracles. The air then gets to the rest of the body through the breathing tubes.
• The sense organs, which are on the outside of the body, pass information to the brain. This is usually in the head, but there are smaller collections of nerves that do some information processing elsewhere in the body.

Scary spiders

Spiders live in almost every part of the world. There are over 60,000 different species, but only about half of them have actually been studied. Spiders are carnivores; they eat insects and other small animals. Most spiders kill their prey by injecting them with poison. They then spray the dead body with digestive juices and suck up the resulting liquid. A row of fine hairs just inside the spider's mouth filters out any lumps. Other spiders don't use poison, but simply spray the trapped insect with digestive juices – they digest the prey to death.

Just a few spiders are dangerous to humans: the black widow, the tarantula, the brown recluse, the funnel web and the red back are some of the scariest spiders on Earth.

Tarantula

spinnerets

abdomen

body
hairs

The poisonous red back is from Australia. Only the female is large enough to bite a person. A victim can become seriously ill.

Red back

The black widow spider is common in Europe and North America and is very poisonous. Its venom is 15 times more poisonous than rattlesnake venom and kills one in every hundred people that it bites.

Black widow

Funnel web

Brown recluse spiders hide in wardrobes and beds. The stinging bite is very painful and the venom kills the skin and muscle around the bite, leaving a hole that takes weeks to heal.

Brown recluse

The funnel web is one of the most dangerous spiders in Australia. The male is more dangerous because he wanders around above ground while the female rarely leaves her funnel-shaped burrow.

Factfile: Spiders
• Spiders have lived on Earth for 400 million years. They were around for about 180 million years before the first dinosaurs.
• Some tarantulas can live for up to 28 years.

Tarantulas (left) are the largest of all spiders. They eat large insects and even small birds and mammals. Although their venom is not fatal to humans, they have large fangs that can give a nasty bite. They can also flick their short body hairs and if these get into the eyes, they can blind.

cephalothorax

eyes

fangs

Orb spider

Orb spiders make wheel webs. This type of web has spokes like a wheel and a sticky thread that spirals around. Making such a complicated and delicate web uses a lot of silk and takes a lot of energy. One species of orb spider can build a web in under an hour using 20 metres of silk.

Spiders use silk to trap their prey. Some keep it simple and make trip wires but most build elaborate webs that catch flying insects with their sticky, almost invisible threads. The silk comes from glands in the spider's abdomen. It starts as liquid and hardens into a gluey thread in the air. It is made of protein, so when the web is damaged the spider eats the silk before making a new one. Spiders also use their silk to wrap up prey to eat later and to make egg-sacs to keep their young safe until they hatch.

To start the web, an orb spider releases a thread. When it sticks to something, the first bridge of the web is formed.

The spider goes up and down the line reinforcing it with extra lines until it is strong. She then produces a thread that hangs down.

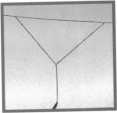

She attaches the loose thread to another point. This Y-shape forms the first three spokes of the web.

Four outer threads are spun to form the frame of the web. These might be attached to twigs or other things nearby.

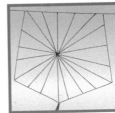

The rest of the spokes are spun and a sticky thread is woven between them to finish the web.

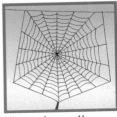

The web usually lasts just one night. In the morning the spider eats it and leaves the main first thread in place.

Factfile: Spiders' webs
• A thread of spider's silk one-hundredth of a millimetre thick can support a weight of 100 grams without breaking.
• Some tropical orb-weaver spiders spin huge webs that stretch more than 5 m across and can snare small birds and bats.

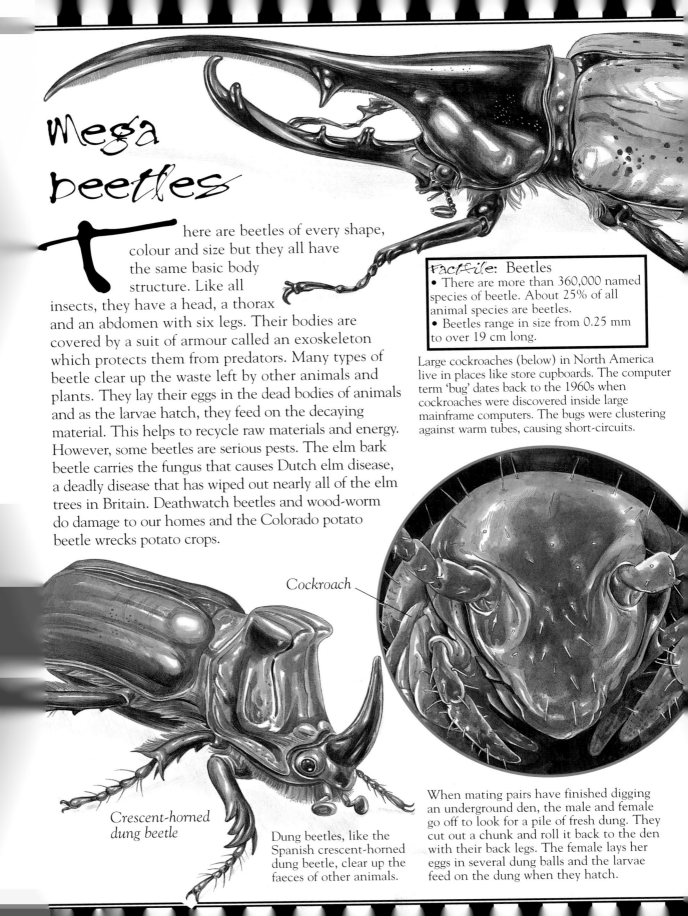

Mega beetles

There are beetles of every shape, colour and size but they all have the same basic body structure. Like all insects, they have a head, a thorax and an abdomen with six legs. Their bodies are covered by a suit of armour called an exoskeleton which protects them from predators. Many types of beetle clear up the waste left by other animals and plants. They lay their eggs in the dead bodies of animals and as the larvae hatch, they feed on the decaying material. This helps to recycle raw materials and energy. However, some beetles are serious pests. The elm bark beetle carries the fungus that causes Dutch elm disease, a deadly disease that has wiped out nearly all of the elm trees in Britain. Deathwatch beetles and wood-worm do damage to our homes and the Colorado potato beetle wrecks potato crops.

Factfile: Beetles
- There are more than 360,000 named species of beetle. About 25% of all animal species are beetles.
- Beetles range in size from 0.25 mm to over 19 cm long.

Large cockroaches (below) in North America live in places like store cupboards. The computer term 'bug' dates back to the 1960s when cockroaches were discovered inside large mainframe computers. The bugs were clustering against warm tubes, causing short-circuits.

Cockroach

Crescent-horned dung beetle

Dung beetles, like the Spanish crescent-horned dung beetle, clear up the faeces of other animals.

When mating pairs have finished digging an underground den, the male and female go off to look for a pile of fresh dung. They cut out a chunk and roll it back to the den with their back legs. The female lays her eggs in several dung balls and the larvae feed on the dung when they hatch.

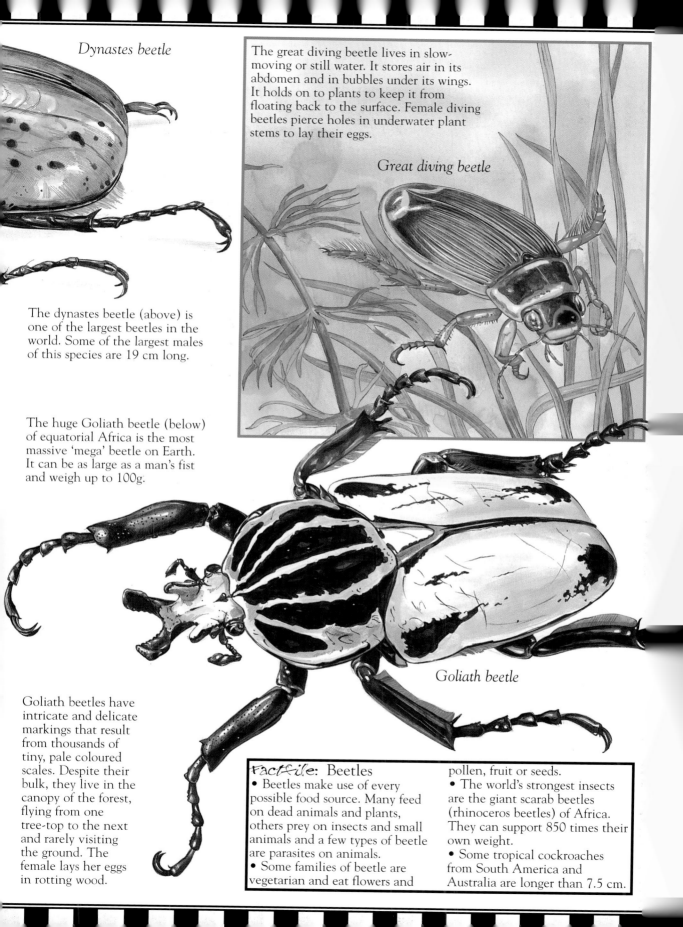

Dynastes beetle

The great diving beetle lives in slow-moving or still water. It stores air in its abdomen and in bubbles under its wings. It holds on to plants to keep it from floating back to the surface. Female diving beetles pierce holes in underwater plant stems to lay their eggs.

Great diving beetle

The dynastes beetle (above) is one of the largest beetles in the world. Some of the largest males of this species are 19 cm long.

The huge Goliath beetle (below) of equatorial Africa is the most massive 'mega' beetle on Earth. It can be as large as a man's fist and weigh up to 100g.

Goliath beetle

Goliath beetles have intricate and delicate markings that result from thousands of tiny, pale coloured scales. Despite their bulk, they live in the canopy of the forest, flying from one tree-top to the next and rarely visiting the ground. The female lays her eggs in rotting wood.

Factfile: Beetles
• Beetles make use of every possible food source. Many feed on dead animals and plants, others prey on insects and small animals and a few types of beetle are parasites on animals.
• Some families of beetle are vegetarian and eat flowers and pollen, fruit or seeds.
• The world's strongest insects are the giant scarab beetles (rhinoceros beetles) of Africa. They can support 850 times their own weight.
• Some tropical cockroaches from South America and Australia are longer than 7.5 cm.

Beautiful butterflies

A dult butterflies have antennae, compound eyes, three pairs of legs, a hard exoskeleton and a body that has three parts: the head, thorax and abdomen. What makes butterflies special is their fragile and stunning beauty. The butterfly's outer body is covered in tiny hairs and the wings are covered by scales. These reflect the light, making the wings glint and change colour. Butterflies are not born this way, they have four stages of life: egg, caterpillar or larva, pupa and adult. They have a life cycle that is described as complete metamorphosis because the caterpillar undergoes a startling change when it pupates. Although the pupa looks dead, there is a lot going on inside. The body of the caterpillar disappears completely and is then re-built from scratch. The result of this 're-building' process is a butterfly that breaks free from its cocoon.

Purple emperor (Apatura iris)

The butterfly troides hypolitus (below) is one of the birdwing butterflies, but it is not as large as the Queen Alexandra birdwing. It was first discovered in 1775.

Troides

Black-veined white

The black-veined white (above right) has striking black veins that give its wings a stained glass appearance. This butterfly was once common all over northern Europe but is now seen very rarely and is probably close to extinction.

What is the difference between a butterfly and a moth? Butterflies are most active during the day, they have clubbed antennae and are brightly coloured. Moths are nocturnal, their antennae are straight and they tend to be drab.

Factfile: Butterflies
• The body lengths of butterflies vary between 1 and 10 cm.
• Wingspan varies between 2 mm and 30 cm. The wingspan of a female Queen Alexandra birdwing can reach 30 cm.

There are over 600 species of swallowtail butterflies in the world. They are brightly coloured to put other insects off eating them, as well as to attract a mate.

Swallowtail

Morphos are large butterflies found in the forests of South America. Males have brightly coloured wings with a metallic sheen that is usually blue but can be red, brown or yellow.

Morpho

The Queen Alexandra birdwing is the largest butterfly in the world and takes about four months to complete its life cycle from egg to adult butterfly. The adult then lives for just three months. Birdwings live in the rainforests of Papua New Guinea but are now very rare.

Male Queen Alexandra birdwings are yellow, green, and/or blue on a black background, while females are brown with lighter spots.

Queen Alexandra birdwing

Factfile: Butterflies
• Butterflies and moths can see ultraviolet light much more easily than humans and so can see patterns on the petals of flowers that we cannot.
• There are approximately 136,800 species of butterflies and moths in the world.

Generating light and sound

Firefly

Some insects really put on a show to attract mates. Glow-worms and fireflies are both beetles that generate their own light. They are nocturnal and communicate with each other using a light organ in the base of their abdomen. Each species of American firefly gives out a unique light signal that only females from the same species can recognise. Insects like crickets, grasshoppers and cicadas prefer to make a noise. Male cicadas spend a lot of time sitting in trees where they 'chirrup' using two plates called tymbals that are found on either side of their abdomen. Two powerful muscles are contracted to make the tymbals vibrate. The tymbals are surrounded by a large airspace inside the shell of the abdomen which acts as an amplifier, making the sound as loud as possible.

Fireflies give out two sorts of light. When resting, they make green flashes, but when flying around, they produce an orange light.

Two chemicals react in a glow-worm's abdomen to give out a bright light. Part of the abdomen is transparent and allows the light to shine through.

Glow-worm

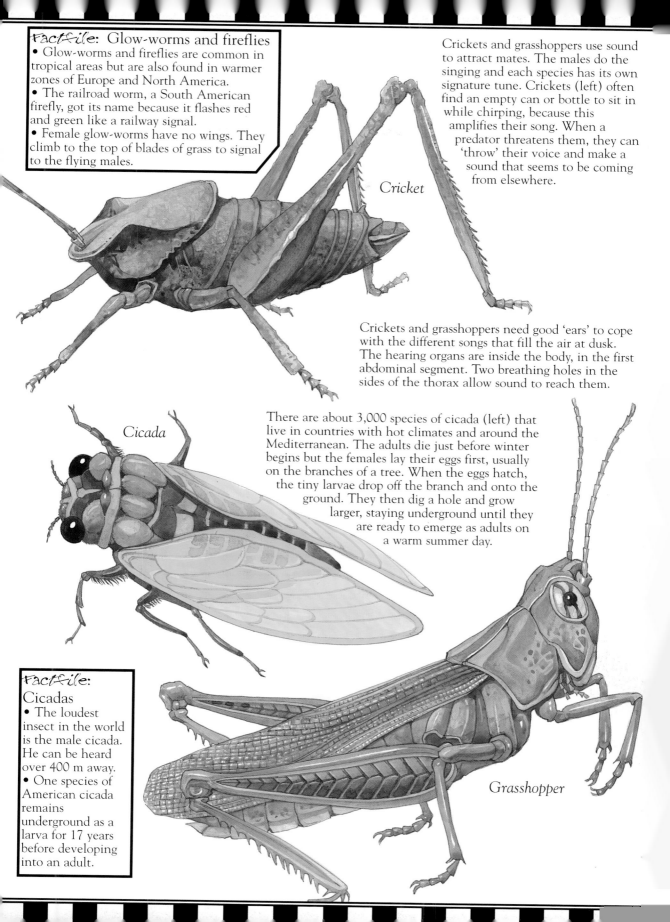

Crickets and grasshoppers use sound to attract mates. The males do the singing and each species has its own signature tune. Crickets (left) often find an empty can or bottle to sit in while chirping, because this amplifies their song. When a predator threatens them, they can 'throw' their voice and make a sound that seems to be coming from elsewhere.

Cricket

Crickets and grasshoppers need good 'ears' to cope with the different songs that fill the air at dusk. The hearing organs are inside the body, in the first abdominal segment. Two breathing holes in the sides of the thorax allow sound to reach them.

Cicada

There are about 3,000 species of cicada (left) that live in countries with hot climates and around the Mediterranean. The adults die just before winter begins but the females lay their eggs first, usually on the branches of a tree. When the eggs hatch, the tiny larvae drop off the branch and onto the ground. They then dig a hole and grow larger, staying underground until they are ready to emerge as adults on a warm summer day.

Grasshopper

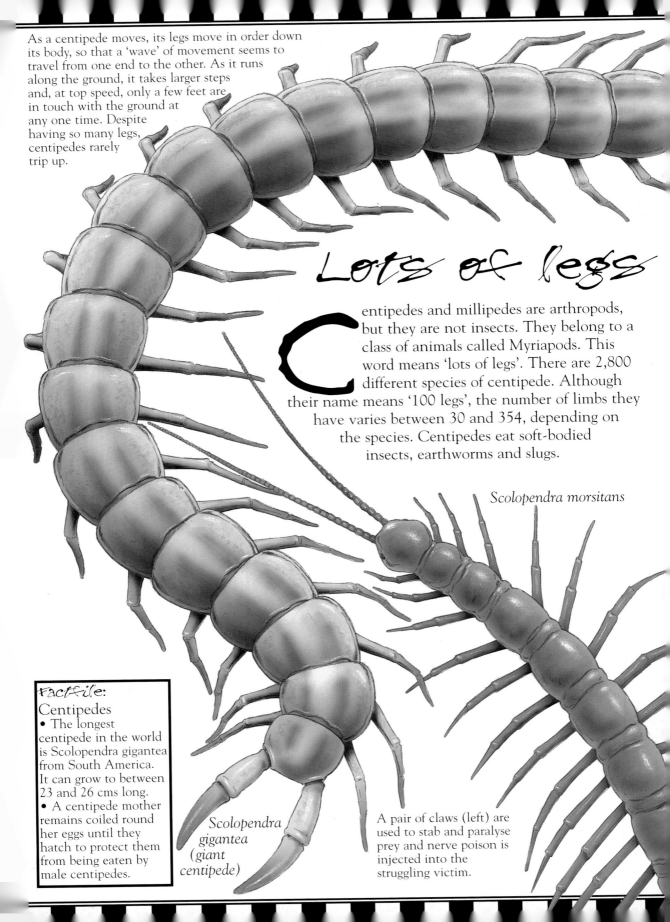

As a centipede moves, its legs move in order down its body, so that a 'wave' of movement seems to travel from one end to the other. As it runs along the ground, it takes larger steps and, at top speed, only a few feet are in touch with the ground at any one time. Despite having so many legs, centipedes rarely trip up.

Lots of legs

Centipedes and millipedes are arthropods, but they are not insects. They belong to a class of animals called Myriapods. This word means 'lots of legs'. There are 2,800 different species of centipede. Although their name means '100 legs', the number of limbs they have varies between 30 and 354, depending on the species. Centipedes eat soft-bodied insects, earthworms and slugs.

Scolopendra morsitans

Factfile:
Centipedes
• The longest centipede in the world is Scolopendra gigantea from South America. It can grow to between 23 and 26 cms long.
• A centipede mother remains coiled round her eggs until they hatch to protect them from being eaten by male centipedes.

Scolopendra gigantea (giant centipede)

A pair of claws (left) are used to stab and paralyse prey and nerve poison is injected into the struggling victim.

The body of a millipede is covered with hard plates of cuticle that overlap, forming tough body armour. The plates are jointed and, when it needs to, the millipede can curl itself into a tight ball (right). Pill millipedes can roll up so well, that no soft tissue is left open to attack by a predator.

Millipede

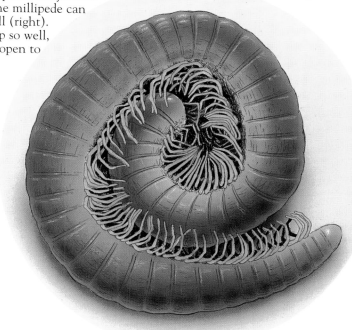

Factfile: Millipedes
• The largest millipede in the world is Graphidostreptus gigas of Africa, which reaches a length of 27 cm and has a body diameter of 2 cm.
• Millipedes usually eat decaying vegetation. Some eat the remains of dead animals and a few tropical species have special long, pointed tubes that they use to pierce fresh fruits and suck out the juice.
• Millipedes live for between 1 and 6 years.
• The millipede Illacme plenipes from California has the most legs of any arthropod – 750!

Millipedes are much gentler creatures than centipedes. They are slower moving and are herbivores – they never hunt. There are about 7,500 known species of millipede. None have as many as a thousand legs, as their name suggests. In fact, millipedes never have more than 750 limbs. Millipedes like hot climates and some species are very sensitive to changes in temperature and moisture. They like to live in damp places, such as soil rich in decomposing leaves.

Centipede   *Millipede*

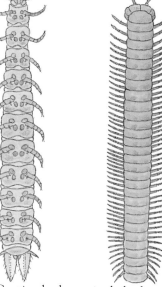

Most of the segments in a millipede's body consist of two segments joined together. The number of segments depends on the species, but most have between 10 and 100 segments. Each segment has two pairs of legs, except the seventh segment which is modified for reproduction purposes.

Centipedes have single body segments with one pair of legs per segment. Millipedes have double segments and two pairs of legs on each one. So, length for length, a millipede has more legs that a centipede.

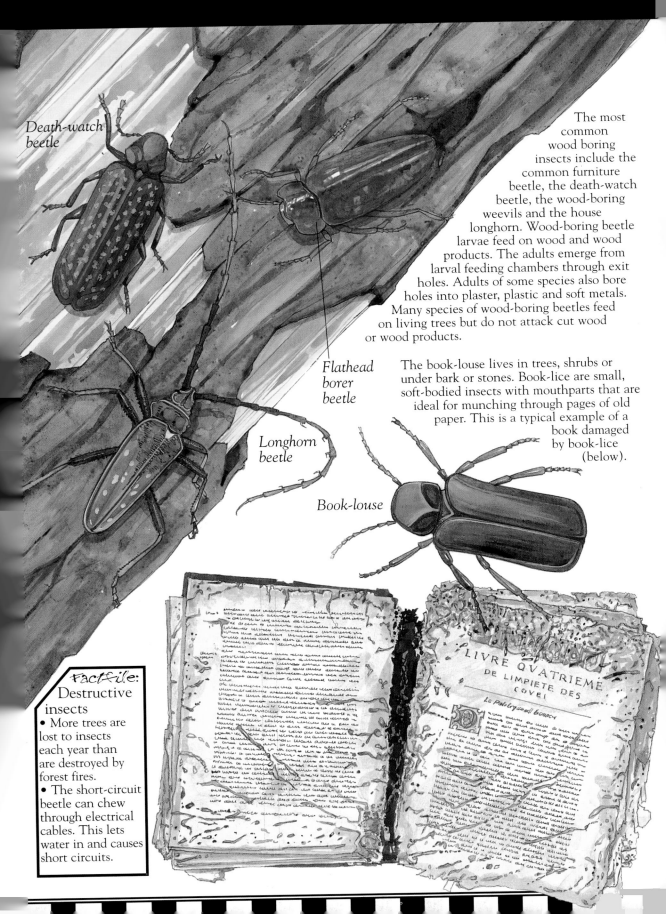

Death-watch beetle

The most common wood boring insects include the common furniture beetle, the death-watch beetle, the wood-boring weevils and the house longhorn. Wood-boring beetle larvae feed on wood and wood products. The adults emerge from larval feeding chambers through exit holes. Adults of some species also bore holes into plaster, plastic and soft metals. Many species of wood-boring beetles feed on living trees but do not attack cut wood or wood products.

Flathead borer beetle

The book-louse lives in trees, shrubs or under bark or stones. Book-lice are small, soft-bodied insects with mouthparts that are ideal for munching through pages of old paper. This is a typical example of a book damaged by book-lice (below).

Longhorn beetle

Book-louse

Factfile:
Destructive insects
• More trees are lost to insects each year than are destroyed by forest fires.
• The short-circuit beetle can chew through electrical cables. This lets water in and causes short circuits.

LIVRE QVATRIEME
DE LIMPIETE DES
COVEI

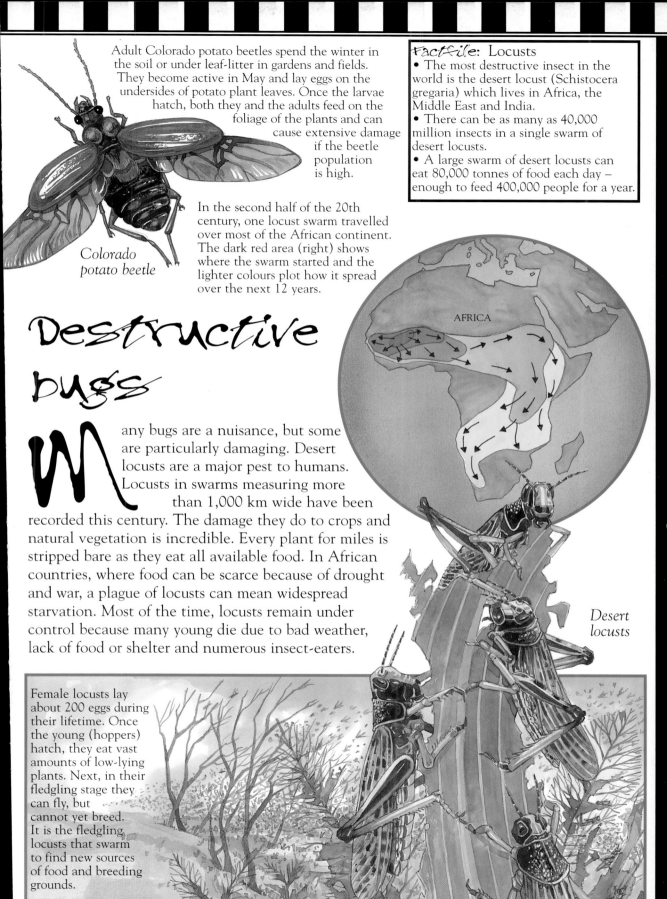

Adult Colorado potato beetles spend the winter in the soil or under leaf-litter in gardens and fields. They become active in May and lay eggs on the undersides of potato plant leaves. Once the larvae hatch, both they and the adults feed on the foliage of the plants and can cause extensive damage if the beetle population is high.

Colorado potato beetle

In the second half of the 20th century, one locust swarm travelled over most of the African continent. The dark red area (right) shows where the swarm started and the lighter colours plot how it spread over the next 12 years.

AFRICA

Destructive bugs

Many bugs are a nuisance, but some are particularly damaging. Desert locusts are a major pest to humans. Locusts in swarms measuring more than 1,000 km wide have been recorded this century. The damage they do to crops and natural vegetation is incredible. Every plant for miles is stripped bare as they eat all available food. In African countries, where food can be scarce because of drought and war, a plague of locusts can mean widespread starvation. Most of the time, locusts remain under control because many young die due to bad weather, lack of food or shelter and numerous insect-eaters.

Desert locusts

Female locusts lay about 200 eggs during their lifetime. Once the young (hoppers) hatch, they eat vast amounts of low-lying plants. Next, in their fledgling stage they can fly, but cannot yet breed. It is the fledgling locusts that swarm to find new sources of food and breeding grounds.

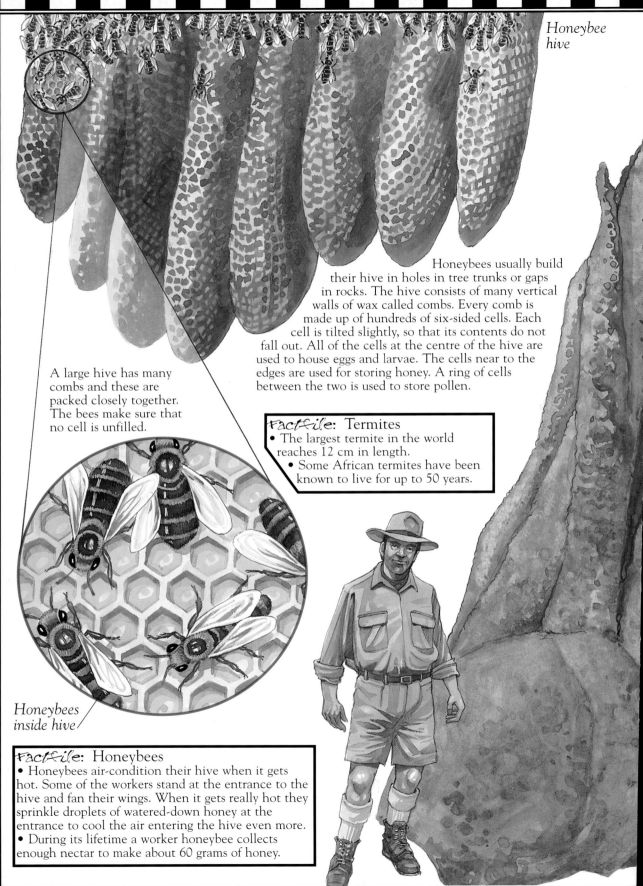

Honeybee hive

Honeybees usually build their hive in holes in tree trunks or gaps in rocks. The hive consists of many vertical walls of wax called combs. Every comb is made up of hundreds of six-sided cells. Each cell is tilted slightly, so that its contents do not fall out. All of the cells at the centre of the hive are used to house eggs and larvae. The cells near to the edges are used for storing honey. A ring of cells between the two is used to store pollen.

A large hive has many combs and these are packed closely together. The bees make sure that no cell is unfilled.

Factfile: Termites
• The largest termite in the world reaches 12 cm in length.
• Some African termites have been known to live for up to 50 years.

Honeybees inside hive

Factfile: Honeybees
• Honeybees air-condition their hive when it gets hot. Some of the workers stand at the entrance to the hive and fan their wings. When it gets really hot they sprinkle droplets of watered-down honey at the entrance to cool the air entering the hive even more.
• During its lifetime a worker honeybee collects enough nectar to make about 60 grams of honey.

The common wasp (right) chews up small pieces of bark from a nearby tree and uses it as a paste to build the walls of its nest. First, they build the horizontal layers and then cover them with an outer shell, leaving a gap at the bottom to get in to lay eggs.

Wasp

Inside a wasp nest

Bug engineers

Some bugs are extremely skilled engineers and builders. Termites, ants and bees live in large colonies and build huge structures to house them and their offspring. These insects are very sociable and they divide up the jobs between them. There is usually one queen, whose job it is to lay all the eggs to keep the colony going. Then there are workers and soldiers. Worker termites are not able to breed because they are sterile. They spend most of their lives underground, looking after the eggs, caring for the young larvae and building, repairing and cleaning the nest. Soldier termites devote themselves to protecting the nest. They are so devoted to this task that they have lost the ability to do anything else – including feeding themselves. They have to be given regurgitated food by the worker termites to stay alive.

Termite mound

Queen termite's chamber

This is a weaver ant nest (below). They usually hang from a tree and are made of leaves stuck together with silk produced by the larvae. Workers operate in teams to squeeze the larvae to make their glands ooze the glue-like silk.

Termites start building their nest underground and then the mound above slowly increases in size. Some of the termite mounds found in Australia are an incredible size – over 13 m high and 30 m in circumference. Termite mounds are very complex inside. They have a central area of horizontal layers in the middle of which is a walled chamber where the queen termite lies, laying thousands of eggs every day.

Weaver ant nest

It's hard being a bug

Many bugs work hard just to survive but there are a few in particular that appear to put in extraordinary effort. Ants, like termites, build large nests that have extremely complicated architecture. The senior ants release chemicals that control worker ants. Under the influence of these chemicals, the workers slave away without rest for most of their lives. Silkmoths produce silk that we use to make clothes and other items and are the only domesticated insect. They have no choice but to work incredibly hard, controlled as they are by humans and dependent on them for survival. The mole cricket is another insect that works hard, but its survival does not depend on human intervention.

Leaf cutter ant

Factfile: Hard workers
• Female mole crickets lay between 200-300 eggs that take 20-30 days to hatch.
• Ant colonies can have as many as one million members.
• Leaf cutter ants do not eat the leaves they collect. They cover them with fungus and suck up the nutrients released as the fungus digests the tough plant material.

abdomen

Mole cricket

The mole cricket is a large burrowing insect that lives underground (right). Its front legs look like those of a mole. The powerful pad-like front feet have large spines that are used to shovel the earth to the sides during burrowing.

Mole crickets have a tough carapace (hood) that protects them from damage as they squeeze through tunnels.

carapace

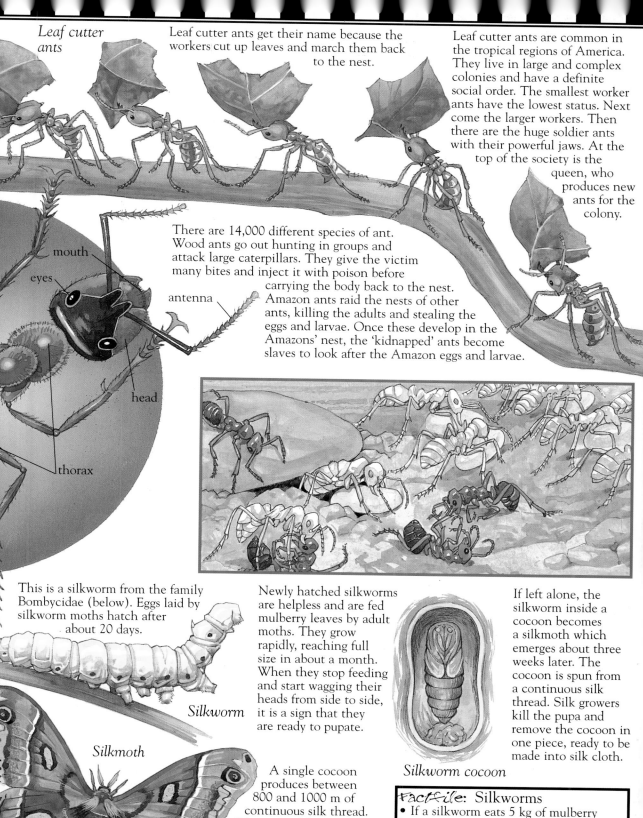

Leaf cutter ants

Leaf cutter ants get their name because the workers cut up leaves and march them back to the nest.

Leaf cutter ants are common in the tropical regions of America. They live in large and complex colonies and have a definite social order. The smallest worker ants have the lowest status. Next come the larger workers. Then there are the huge soldier ants with their powerful jaws. At the top of the society is the queen, who produces new ants for the colony.

mouth

eyes

antenna

head

thorax

There are 14,000 different species of ant. Wood ants go out hunting in groups and attack large caterpillars. They give the victim many bites and inject it with poison before carrying the body back to the nest. Amazon ants raid the nests of other ants, killing the adults and stealing the eggs and larvae. Once these develop in the Amazons' nest, the 'kidnapped' ants become slaves to look after the Amazon eggs and larvae.

This is a silkworm from the family Bombycidae (below). Eggs laid by silkworm moths hatch after about 20 days.

Silkworm

Silkmoth

Newly hatched silkworms are helpless and are fed mulberry leaves by adult moths. They grow rapidly, reaching full size in about a month. When they stop feeding and start wagging their heads from side to side, it is a sign that they are ready to pupate.

If left alone, the silkworm inside a cocoon becomes a silkmoth which emerges about three weeks later. The cocoon is spun from a continuous silk thread. Silk growers kill the pupa and remove the cocoon in one piece, ready to be made into silk cloth.

Silkworm cocoon

A single cocoon produces between 800 and 1000 m of continuous silk thread. This seems like a lot but about 50,000 silkworms are killed to make one kilogram of raw silk.

Factfile: Silkworms
• If a silkworm eats 5 kg of mulberry leaves, it can make enough silk to spin into a thread more than 160 km long.
• Silkmoths are one of the largest moths in the world: they have a wingspan of over 30 cm.

Magnificent mothers

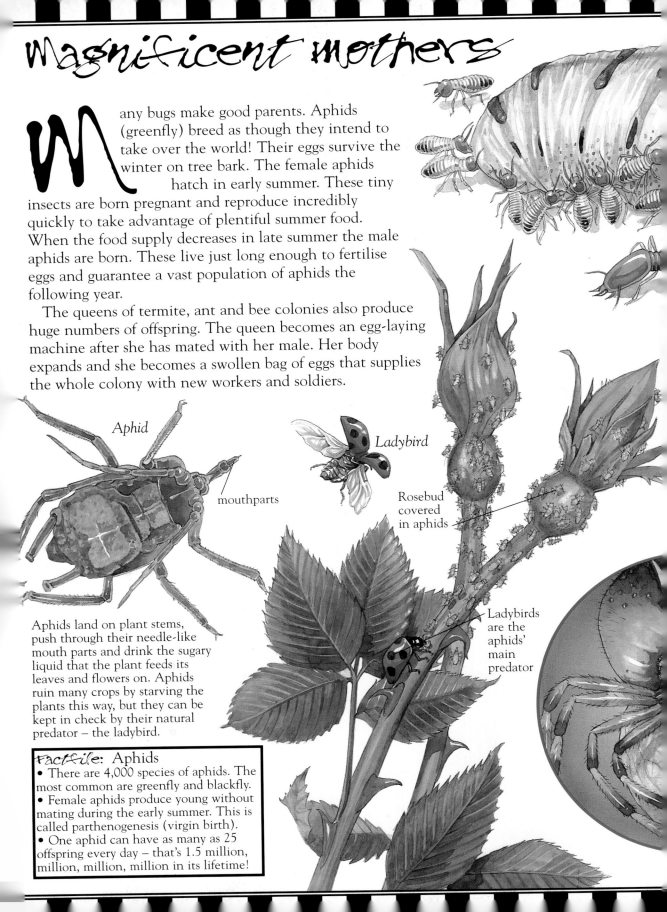

Many bugs make good parents. Aphids (greenfly) breed as though they intend to take over the world! Their eggs survive the winter on tree bark. The female aphids hatch in early summer. These tiny insects are born pregnant and reproduce incredibly quickly to take advantage of plentiful summer food. When the food supply decreases in late summer the male aphids are born. These live just long enough to fertilise eggs and guarantee a vast population of aphids the following year.

The queens of termite, ant and bee colonies also produce huge numbers of offspring. The queen becomes an egg-laying machine after she has mated with her male. Her body expands and she becomes a swollen bag of eggs that supplies the whole colony with new workers and soldiers.

Aphid

mouthparts

Ladybird

Rosebud covered in aphids

Ladybirds are the aphids' main predator

Aphids land on plant stems, push through their needle-like mouth parts and drink the sugary liquid that the plant feeds its leaves and flowers on. Aphids ruin many crops by starving the plants this way, but they can be kept in check by their natural predator – the ladybird.

Factfile: Aphids
- There are 4,000 species of aphids. The most common are greenfly and blackfly.
- Female aphids produce young without mating during the early summer. This is called parthenogenesis (virgin birth).
- One aphid can have as many as 25 offspring every day – that's 1.5 million, million, million, million in its lifetime!

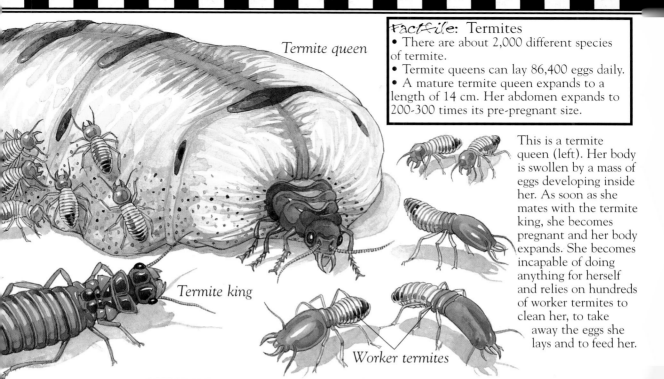

Termite queen

This is a termite queen (left). Her body is swollen by a mass of eggs developing inside her. As soon as she mates with the termite king, she becomes pregnant and her body expands. She becomes incapable of doing anything for herself and relies on hundreds of worker termites to clean her, to take away the eggs she lays and to feed her.

Termite king

Worker termites

Wolf spider mothers put their eggs in a sac of silk (below) and attach the sac behind their body. After the young hatch, the female carries them for a while on her abdomen. Often she will care for her youngsters until she dies.

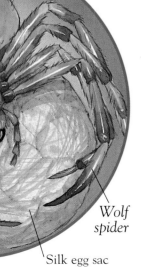

Wolf spider

Silk egg sac

The mating behaviour of spiders differs widely between species. Mating can be a dangerous business for the male. Quite often, the female eats him once mating is over. So, spiders that are surrounded by their babies are almost always female.

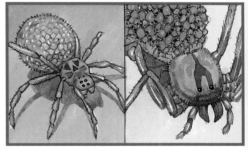

Once the eggs are fertilised, they mature in the female's body before she lays them. Spider mothers take great care of their offspring. They often carry the eggs or the young on their abdomen so that the weather or predators cannot harm them.

Many spider mothers put their eggs in a sac of silk and guard them until they hatch. A few species of spider produce offspring who eat their mother shortly after emerging from their carefully protected nursery.

The eggs of Araneus diadematus are laid in a ball, in plant stems. When they are ready to hatch, a slight touch, caused by an animal or a breeze, causes the ball to explode, releasing the tiny spiders in all directions.

Unwanted passengers

Dog flea

Some bugs are parasites and pests. They live on other animals, sucking their blood and using them for warmth and shelter. This is fine for the bug, but the host, the animal it makes its victim, is not so lucky. The bites of mosquitoes, fleas and ticks can be very painful and can get infected. Worst of all, the bites can pass on deadly diseases such as malaria. Bugs that bite us live with us, in our clothes, in our beds and in our hair. Getting rid of them can be very difficult and being clean is no guarantee that we will escape their attentions.

Factfile: Parasites and pests
• The largest flea in the world is Hystrichopsylla scheffleri. It can be as big as 11 mm long and 8 mm wide.
• There are 3,150 species of lice that live on other creatures. They have been on Earth for 130 million years.
• The eggs of a human head-louse are known as 'nits'.
• Assassin bugs can bite people, and in South America their bites spread a deadly disease.

Dog and cat fleas do not live on people, but they can bite them, leaving an itchy spot. Only human lice can pass disease between people. The worst case happened in Russia between 1918 and 1922 when 3 million people died after catching a disease spread by lice.

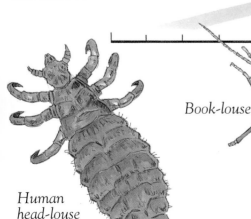

Human head-louse

Book-louse

Bedbug

Human head-lice have no wings and cannot fly. They jump from head to head and cling to their hosts using well-developed claws on the ends of their legs. Head-lice bites cause intense itching.

Book-lice feed on the mould that grows in old, damp books and damage the paper in the process. The full name of the common book-louse is Liposcelis divinatorius.

Bedbugs feed on human blood and live in mattresses and bedding. Normally about 6 mm long, they expand to 3 or 4 times their normal size because of the blood in their gut.

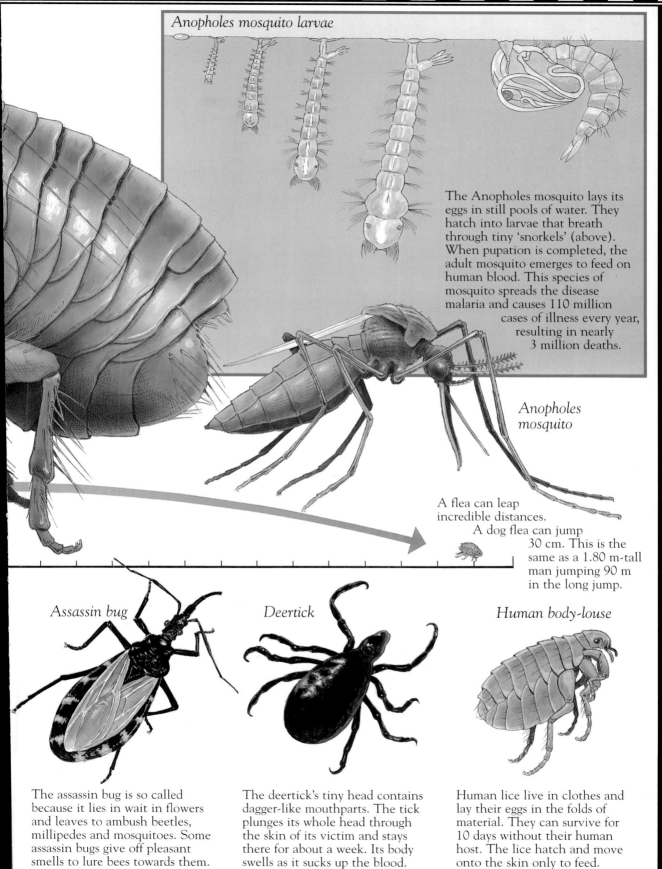

Anopholes mosquito larvae

The Anopholes mosquito lays its eggs in still pools of water. They hatch into larvae that breath through tiny 'snorkels' (above). When pupation is completed, the adult mosquito emerges to feed on human blood. This species of mosquito spreads the disease malaria and causes 110 million cases of illness every year, resulting in nearly 3 million deaths.

Anopholes mosquito

A flea can leap incredible distances. A dog flea can jump 30 cm. This is the same as a 1.80 m-tall man jumping 90 m in the long jump.

Assassin bug

The assassin bug is so called because it lies in wait in flowers and leaves to ambush beetles, millipedes and mosquitoes. Some assassin bugs give off pleasant smells to lure bees towards them.

Deertick

The deertick's tiny head contains dagger-like mouthparts. The tick plunges its whole head through the skin of its victim and stays there for about a week. Its body swells as it sucks up the blood.

Human body-louse

Human lice live in clothes and lay their eggs in the folds of material. They can survive for 10 days without their human host. The lice hatch and move onto the skin only to feed.

Invisible bugs

All bugs have predators – enemies that want to eat them. Different types of arthropods have developed various strategies to avoid being caught. Some live in colonies in elaborate nests, going out as little as possible. Others have strong defences – perhaps fierce mouthparts and venom. Still others contain bad-tasting chemicals or poison that make them impossible to eat. The bugs on these two pages have a more subtle approach – they blend into the background so that predators look straight past them. So effective are their disguises that you might have trouble spotting them yourself. Have a look – every bug mentioned is illustrated somewhere on the page.

Geomantis larvoides

The mantis Geomantis larvoides (above) has evolved to look like a piece of old wood. It is not as glamorous as many of the other mantises, but it is easily mistaken for a seed pod, or a dead twig or leaf and so escapes predators very well.

Praying mantis

The common European praying mantis lives among leafy branches and on blades of grass. Its stick-like green body helps it to camouflage itself from predators. It gets its name because its two front limbs are always slightly bent and it looks as though it is kneeling to pray.

Crestal mantis

This mantis mimics the appearance of broad green leaves. When prey is close enough, the mantis's attack is quick and deadly. The neck of the prey is chewed to paralyse it and then the mantis eats the rest of the body.

Lappet moth

Lappet moths look like autumn leaves. The larvae feed on poplar, aspen and willow trees and are common in Canada. They spend the winter as pupae and hatch into moths the following spring.

Factfile: Mantises
• A Sri Lankan species of mantis called Heirodula grows to a length of 25 cm.
• Female praying mantises often eat the male during mating.
• Although they don't look very similar, mantises are closely related to cockroaches.

Stick insect

The giant stick insect, usually known as the walking-stick, eats the leaves of oaks and other hardwoods. It escapes predators by looking exactly like the twigs that it sits on. Adults are between 62-76 mm long and their body colour can be brown, green, grey or red.

Leaf insect

Some stick insects, rather than imitating twigs and sticks, have developed to look like the leaves in which they hide. The body and legs of a leaf insect look very realistic. The edges of its body even look as though an animal has chewed them.

Orchid mantis

The orchid mantis has one of the most fantastic disguises of all. Its body is elaborately folded and the swollen and strongly coloured limbs make it appear exactly like the exotic orchids that cover its local vegetation.

Factfile: Stick insects
• The world's longest insect is the tropical stick insect Pharnacia serratipes, which reaches a length of 35 cm.
• Some tropical walking-sticks can change colour because of changes in humidity, light intensity and temperature.

BUG QUIZ

1. To which section of an insect are the legs attached?
a) The head.
b) The thorax.
c) The abdomen.

2. What percentage of all the animals in the world are beetles?
a) 25%
b) 50%
c) 5%

3. What is the wingspan of an adult female Queen Alexandra birdwing?
a) About 13 cm.
b) About 30 cm.
c) About 60 cm.

4. How long do American cicada larvae live underground?
a) 17 weeks.
b) 17 months.
c) 17 years.

5. What is the maximum number of legs a millipede can have?
a) 750
b) 1000
c) 100

6. What are the most destructive insects in the world?
a) Locusts
b) Furniture beetles
c) Book-lice

7. What do silkworms eat?
a) Gooseberry leaves.
b) Blackberry leaves.
c) Mulberry leaves.

8. What type of insect is born pregnant?
a) The termite queen.
b) The female aphid.
c) The queen bee.

9. How many eggs does a termite queen lay every day?
a) 46,800
b) 64,800
c) 86,400

10. What part of a plant do walking-stick insects look like?
a) A twig.
b) A leaf.
c) A flower.

Quiz answers are on page 32.

Glossary

abdomen The part of the body of an arthropod that usually contains the digestive system and reproduction organs.

arachnid A sub-group of the arthropods that includes spiders.

arthropod The class of animals that includes insects, spiders, centipedes and millipedes. Arthropods do not have a backbone and they have a tough exoskeleton. Their bodies are divided into sections. In insects there are three: the head, thorax and abdomen.

carnivore An animal that kills other animals for food.

cephalothorax In spiders, this word describes the head and thorax, which are fused together.

cocoon The silk casing in which a butterfly or moth pupates.

complete metamorphosis This means 'complete change' and describes a life cycle in which the larva pupates when it has grown big enough. The larva and the adult stages of the life cycle usually look completely different.

compound eye An eye made up of numerous units. Compound eyes usually have many lenses unlike a human eye which only contains one.

cuticle The outer layer of an arthropod exoskeleton that protects the body from drying out.

dorsal The back parts of an animal. The red and black markings on a ladybird, for example, can be seen on its dorsal surface.

exoskeleton The outer, hard armour that supports and protects the body of an arthropod.

incomplete metamorphosis This means 'incomplete change' and describes a life cycle in which an egg hatches into a nymph. It does not pupate.

invertebrate An animal that does not have a backbone. All insects, spiders, centipedes and millipedes are invertebrates.

larvae Larvae are young forms of the animal that do not look like the adult. Some arthropods hatch from eggs into larvae before becoming a pupa. A caterpillar, for example, is the larva of a butterfly.

nocturnal An animal that is more active in the night than in the day is said to be nocturnal. Most moths are nocturnal.

nymph Some arthropods hatch from eggs into nymphs. These are young forms of the animal that look exactly like small versions of the adult.

parthenogenesis A method of reproduction without fertilization.

phylum A name given to sub-divisions within the animal kingdom. Phylums help scientists identify animals more easily.

predator An animal that hunts another animal for food.

prey An animal that is hunted by another animal for food.

proboscis The part of an insect's mouthparts that resembles a tongue.

pupa During complete metamorphosis, the larva binds itself into a pupa, or cocoon. After pupating for a few days, the adult emerges.

scavenger An animal that feeds on the bodies of animals that are already dead. Scavengers do not hunt or kill animals themselves.

spiracle An opening on the outside of an insect's body for breathing through.

thorax The middle body section of an insect. The legs and wings are usually attached to the thorax.

venom Another word for poison.

ventral The underside of an animal's body is called its ventral surface.

Index